IF FOU

MW01147370

Greater Than a Tourist Book Series
Reviews from Readers

I think the series is wonderful and beneficial for tourists to get information before visiting the city.

-Seckin Zumbul, Izmir Turkey

I am a world traveler who has read many trip guides but this one really made a difference for me. I would call it a heartfelt creation of a local guide expert instead of just a guide.

-Susy, Isla Holbox, Mexico

New to the area like me, this is a must have!

-Joe, Bloomington, USA

This is a good series that gets down to it when looking for things to do at your destination without having to read a novel for just a few ideas.

-Rachel, Monterey, USA

GREATER THAN A TOURIST- ALASKA USA

50 Travel Tips from a Local

Phylicia Hanson-Stitzel

Cover designed by: Ivana Stamenkovic
Cover Image: https://pixabay.com/en/landscape-mountains-snow-denali-1757152/

CZYK Publishing Since 2011.

Greater Than a Tourist
Visit our website at www.GreaterThanaTourist.com

Lock Haven, PA
ISBN: 9781793123404

>TOURIST

50 TRAVEL TIPS FROM A LOCAL

BOOK DESCRIPTION

Are you excited about planning your next trip?

Do you want to try something new?

Would you like some guidance from a local?

If you answered yes to any of these questions, then this Greater Than a Tourist book is for you.

Greater Than a Tourist- Alaska by Phylicia Hanson-Stitzel offers the inside scoop on Alaska. Most travel books tell you how to travel like a tourist. Although there is nothing wrong with that, as part of the Greater Than a Tourist series, this book will give you travel tips from someone who has lived at your next travel destination.

In these pages, you will discover advice that will help you throughout your stay. This book will not tell you exact addresses or store hours but instead will give you excitement and knowledge from a local that you may not find in other smaller print travel books.

Travel like a local. Slow down, stay in one place, and get to know the people and the culture. By the time you finish this book, you will be eager and prepared to travel to your next destination.

TABLE OF CONTENTS

16. Tour of the Arctic Circle from Fairbanks

17. Dog Sledding and Kennel

18. Running Reindeer Ranch

19. Antler Arch

20. Downtown Fairbanks

21. Take A Ride Through History!

22. Frozen Sleep at the Ice Hotel

23. Midnight Sun Festival

24. Golden Days Festival

25. Fairbanks Summer Arts Festival

26. WEIO! (World Eskimo-Indian Olympics)

27. Take A Flight to Our Capital!

28. Exit Glacier Hike

29. Winner Creek Hike

30. Inside Passage

31. Sitka

32. Ketchikan

33. Skagway

34. Watch the salmon run at Pullen Creek

35. Hike to Yakutania Point and Smuggler's Cove

36. White Pass & Yukon Route Railway

37. Kroschel Films Wildlife Center

38. Kodiak Island, Kodiak

39. Alutiiq Museum – Kodiak

40. Kodiak Military History Museum

41. Kodiak Wildlife Tours

DEDICATION

This book is dedicated to my wonderful husband, Peter, who has always encouraged me in whatever crazy dream I peruse. And to my family, most of whom still live in my home town and state, if it weren't for you guys, I never would have become who I am today and for that I am thankful!

ABOUT THE AUTHOR

Phylicia, who was born and raised in the greatest state of Alaska currently is attached to her husband, who is active duty Navy, so they get moved around a lot. Phylicia is a photojournalist by trade and earned her Bachelor of Science in Photography and Photojournalism. Phylicia grew up with a strong influence to travel from her mom, who took her on countless adventures around the world and across the United States during her adolescence. Phylicia continues that tradition with her own daughter, who has more visa stamps than a good portion of adults before the age two.

HOW TO USE THIS BOOK

The Greater Than a Tourist book series was written by someone who has lived in an area for over three months. The goal of this book is to help travelers either dream or experience different locations by providing opinions from a local. The author has made suggestions based on their own experiences. Please do your own research before traveling to the area in case the suggested places are unavailable.

Travel Advisories: As a first step in planning any trip abroad, check the Travel Advisories for your intended destination.
https://travel.state.gov/content/travel/en/traveladvisories/traveladvisories.html

FROM THE PUBLISHER

Traveling can be one of the most important parts of a person's life. The anticipation and memories that you have are some of the best. As a publisher of the Greater Than a Tourist book series, as well as the popular 50 Things to Know book series, we strive to help you learn about new places, spark your imagination, and inspire you. Wherever you are and whatever you do I wish you safe, fun, and inspiring travel.

Lisa Rusczyk Ed. D.
CZYK Publishing

OUR STORY

Traveling is a passion of the "Greater than a Tourist" series creator. Lisa studied abroad in college, and for their honeymoon Lisa and her husband toured Europe. During her travels to Malta, an older man tried to give her some advice based on his own experience living on the island since he was a young boy. She was not sure if she should talk to the stranger but was interested in his advice. When traveling to some places she was wary to talk to locals because she was afraid that they weren't being genuine. Through her travels, Lisa learned how much locals had to share with tourists. Lisa created the "Greater Than a Tourist" book series to help connect people with locals. A topic that locals are very passionate about sharing.

WELCOME TO
> TOURIST

*"Nobody is accidentally in
Alaska. The people who are in
Alaska are there because they
choose to be, so they've sort of got a
real frontier ethic."*

- Marcus Sakey

1. "ALASKA IS ON MY BUCKET LIST"

Growing up in Alaska, you can imagine that it can be a little isolated from the world around us. I mean, come on, it takes three days to drive through Canada. But my mom was always very diligent to take us on trips, so whenever we traveled around the world, you generally get asked "so where are you from?" When I tell them I am from Alaska the first thing I always hear "OH! Alaska! I so want to go there! It's on my bucket list"

Well that is an excellent answer because in this book you will be able to read about all the best places to go in Alaska, the best ways to travel and even when to schedule out your trip! Ready? Let's dig in!

13

2. WHEN IS THE BEST TIME TO GO?

In my humble opinion, Alaska is beautiful all year round. However, there are highlight times of the year that are the best times to visit depending on what you'd like to see.

If you can handle the cold, Alaska won't disappoint you. It shouldn't come as any surprise, but the Northern lights draw a ton of people to Alaska. I know, big shock, right? The best time to view the Aurora Borealis is between the months of December and February. That is when the temperature plumages. The colder the night the better the Borealis show.

Then about six months later, June and July are the best summer months to come and visit the Last Frontier. If you are looking to play in the midnight sun these are the best times to come and visit. So now you can start planning your trip.

3. FJORDS AND GLACIERS

Alaska has an endless number of glaciers and fjords to visit. Hubbard Glacier which was first mapped in 1895, Mandenhall Glacier in Juneau, Kenai Fjords National Park, Tracy Arm Fjord in Juneau, Holgate Glacier in Seward and Kachemak Bay State Park and so much more. Each of these locations you could spend an hour, a day even a week exploring around, hiking, kayaking, sledding, the list goes on and on.

4. DENALI NATIONAL PARK

This is a spot where I recommend every spends at least three days. Roughly 400,000 travelers make it to and through Denali every year between the months of May and September, during the main summer months. But I believe the best time to visit is in the fall when all of the caribou are migrating through the park. The fall colors don't last long but when the colors sprout driving through the park is an unforgettable experience.

There are also rapids that can be rode, small shops for shopping and amazing restaurants that have breath-taking views.

5. "MY HOMETOWN" FAIRBANKS – THE GOLDEN HEART

Fairbanks is known as the "Golden Heart City" of Alaska. The nickname captures Fairbanks perfectly. We are a hugely hearted community and Fairbanks is a large gathering location for a lot of the surround villages. The Chief Andrew Isaac health center, the Chief Peter John Tribal Building and the David Salmon Tribal Hall are all major assets to the Native communities.

6. PIONEER PARK – BETTER KNOWN AS "ALASKA LAND"

Alaska Land (a name still used by locals), now renamed Pioneer park, is a great place to spend the day in Fairbanks. The park is free so it's a great place to save money and still learn about Alaska's tough history through grueling winters that dropped below -80°F or about the strategic military advantage the

United States had because of rural outposts and brave Bush pilots in WWII. There are also lots of shopping and food cabins. Each of the cabins you'll see around the park are original structures from when settlers came to Fairbanks, so even shopping is a historical trip.

7. THE GREAT ICEBERG!

Spend the afternoon wondering around University of Alaska Museum of the North. The locals joke about with tourists when giving directions and say "take a left at the iceberg", this isn't Alaskans being rude, the architectural design was based on one of the Alaska's many icebergs that we have floating off the coast of Barrow. This came about because this where a lot of teams that submit their research into the museum are based close to Barrow. This museum is also the ONLY research and teaching museum in the state of Alaska.

These collections form the foundation for the museum's research, education programs, and exhibits. Highlights include a 2,000-year spectrum of Alaska art, from ancient ivory carvings to contemporary paintings and sculpture, in the Rose Berry Alaska Art; the state's largest public display of gold and Blue Babe, an almost 50,000-year-old mummified steppe bison, and an ever-changing sound and light installation driven by the real-time positions of the sun and moon, seismic activity, and the aurora.

8. GOLD DREDGE NO. 8

Goldstream Dredge No. 8 is a ladder dredge operated by the Fairbanks Exploration Company from 1928 to 1959. It is located on the old Steese Highway between Fairbanks and Fox (where I grew up). Starting in the 1920s, water was brought to the area through the 90-mile Davidson Ditch for gold mining.

This is a summer activity, only open to tourists between May and September so make sure you check their website, they also book up fast during the summer so book this tour out early to ensure that you get a chance to PAN FOR GOLD! Yes - you keep any gold you find, I've found several flakes myself!

9. ALYESKA PIPELINE VIEWING

This next stop is a major point of pride for me. When you leave Gold Dredge No. 8 you can take a veer from the Old Steese and get a close-up look at one of the world's engineering marvels. I am particular to showing off this location because my Grandfather was one of the designing engineers on the project. Here you will find informational displays about the pipeline and you'll see Alaska's Pig and stand amazed at the engineering feat it took to build the Alyeska Pipeline. You can visit this location all year-round and is a nice 30-45-minute info stop.

10. RIVERBOAT DISCOVERY

There are some things, when you travel, that you can't do without being a tourist. This is something I had to accept long ago because governments or businesses have cut off individual access and the only way to see or experience the location is to hop on a tour. The Riverboat Discovery will float you up the Chena River where you will see a sled dog training camp that is owned by Susan Baker's descendants who are still running the training program the same

19

way she did, then you'll see a bush plane land and take off right from the river to give you an insight to what it is like living out in the villages where all of their food and supplies are flown in on these bush planes. That demonstration is well timed because shortly after the plane takes off you will dock and get off the boat at a recreated fish camp where you'll learn about the history and traditions that are still used today by the Athabaskan people. You will be able to stretch your legs as you walk around the villages with the hunting huts. Then you will board the ship again and return to Fairbanks.

11. CHENA HOT SPRINGS

It is always good to have options and if you like lots of options Chena Hot Springs is the place for you. If you wanted to make a half day, full day, weekend, or an entire week Chena hot springs has what you need. A full range of summer and winter activities you can book through their activities counter is just the start of all the things you can experience spending time at Chena. Of course, the first draw is the hot springs themselves. This is a great place to soak up relaxing minerals from the springs – if you make a trip in the winter this is one of the most famous locations where you can view the Northern Lights! And of course, what better way to do so than while soaking in the hot springs?

There are also great overnight options, in 2005 a hotel was built to start accommodating the inflicts of tourists, but if you want to bunker down in a cozy cottage there are "spring side" cabins. If you are road tripping – we got something

12. ANGEL ROCKS TRAILS

Located near Chena Hot Springs Angel Rocks this is a wonderful hike for those who are outdoors or athletically inclined. You could spend two hours or a whole afternoon out on the trails hiking to the top of Angel Rocks or one of the shorter trails surrounding the area.

13. CREAMERS FIELD MIGRATORY WATERFOWL REFUGE

Creamer's Field Migratory Waterfowl Refuge is a 2,000-acre refuge on the site of the historic Creamer's Dairy in Fairbanks, Alaska. The Dairy was once the largest producer in Alaska and is on the historic registry of places. The refuge has miles of multi-use trails that are open year-round, and it is an excellent location for bird watching and wildlife viewing. The Farmhouse Visitor Center & Gift Shop is open daily in the summer from 9:30 - 5 and on Saturdays in the winter from Noon - 4. Guided Nature Walks are available Mon-Sat at 10 am June through August by trained naturalists. In the winter the trails are groomed for cross country skiing and skijoring. Dog mushers, walkers and runners also visit the fields and trails regularly. During the migration seasons the fields are closed except to the birds, but the other trails are still open away from the fields. Come visit!

14. GOLDEN HEART PLAZA

Staged in the middle of downtown Fairbanks. The "First Family" statue is in the middle of the fountain, which is in the middle of a plaza that is used for many events throughout the year. Farmer's markets, music, and various downtown celebrations all utilize the space. It is always good to just stop by and see what is going on in the Plaza.

15. ALASKAN HUSKY AND HORSE ADVENTURES

I know, what a crazy combination! But this is one of the most unique things you could do while visiting Alaska. They offer summer adventure tours with horses from 1 hour to 10 days camping on the trail, stunning scenery and in winter they offer the same caliber trips but with sled dogs!

16. TOUR OF THE ARCTIC CIRCLE FROM FAIRBANKS

For those travelers who are looking to check another location off their bucket list, this is the place to go! It is a full day drive or you can take a weekend tour but I would highly suggest taking this trip. You get to see a lot of very cool scenes of Alaska but you also get to travel to one of the greatest places on earth!

17. DOG SLEDDING AND KENNEL

Immerse yourself in the quintessential Alaskan sport of a dog mushing adventure. There are several tours who pick you up at your hotel in Fairbanks, you'll visit a local kennel and take a tour with a professional dog musher, who will introduce you to your team of Husky sled dogs. Then, sit beneath a blanket while you sled over hills and through forests of spruce trees on a thrilling excursion that is rich in Alaskan history. This is the truest Alaskan experience you can have during your visit!

18. RUNNING REINDEER RANCH

OPEN BY APPOINTMENT ONLY, NO DROP-INS ACCOMMODATED. PLEASE CALL FIRST. Enjoy a walk through the boreal forest of Alaska with our curious and gentle reindeer. See the reindeer romp free through the forest doing "reindeery" things. After the walk you will return to the house for a light refreshment and to finish up the conversation. What I love about this location is that every time I've gone to visit, each time is different. They are open year-round by appointment only. Same day reservations sometimes available but you must contact us in advance. The running joke is that the winter cut off temperature -65 F. (That's a joke, it really never gets that cold! Well…it has but the likely of it is EXTREMELY low.)

19. ANTLER ARCH

This arch is located at the Morris Thompson Center in Fairbanks, it isn't a major location but it is a little hidden gem that is always good for a photo to show a little local culture.

20. DOWNTOWN FAIRBANKS

Starting on 1st Ave in downtown Fairbanks at the Golden Heart Plaza the best way to experience downtown is to wander. Between 1st and 4th Ave there are a lot of little shops, local museums and great places to grab a bite to eat! Definitely a great way to spend a beautiful afternoon!

21. TAKE A RIDE THROUGH HISTORY!

One of the gems of Fairbanks is the Railroad! I know, it doesn't seem like this would be a gem, but this is a fantastic way that you can see the beauty of Alaska without ever having to get behind the wheel and try to navigate your way.

A great day trip to make is from Fairbanks to Denali, you can board the train in the "industrial" area of Fairbanks, with the newly built train depot, and spend the afternoon relaxing and taking in all the beautiful sights of Alaska as the train takes you through the mountains of the Alaska Range. During your trip you will hear about some of the great pieces of Alaskan History. For instance, about 50 miles south of Fairbanks you will reach the town of Nenana, located on the meeting of the Nenana and Tanana Rivers. As you approach town you will cross over the Tanana River, a 700 foot long steel bridge, one of the longest single span bridges in the world, as well as the site where President Warren G Harding drove in the final ceremonial gold spike in 1923 at the completion of the Alaska Railroad. This is just one of the nuggets of history you will receive while riding the train – keep your eyes peeled for wildlife.

Don't think that you only can take the train to Denali, the railroad offers several options for trips you can take throughout Alaska. However, if you are looking for a good day or even weekend trip to our great mountain this is the best way to go!

22. FROZEN SLEEP AT THE ICE HOTEL

Sounds like a chilly night doesn't it? The Ice Hotel, located out at Chena Hot Springs, isn't for sleeping quarters anymore. When it first opened the rooms were reserved for high-end clients wanting an Alaskan experience in June however, now it is a museum where you can bundle up in fur coats, (if you are over the age of 21) can get a martini out of an ice glass and stand under the roof in awe of the ice creation around you.

Ice carving is very famous in Alaska, especially in Fairbanks. The International Ice Carving Competition is held in Fairbanks every year, plan your trip for the end of February to the first two weeks in March if you would like to behold this international phenomenon!

As you walk through the Ice Hotel, you can see the rooms with beds made of ice, beautiful banisters and for a laugh you can even get a picture inside the ice outhouse that is located inside the "master" bedroom. Everything in the museum is made of ice other than the fur rugs you see for decoration and some wood laid down to ensure you don't slip and fall on your behind.

FAIRBANKS FESTIVALS:

23. MIDNIGHT SUN FESTIVAL

Alaska is always thought of to be dark, cold and covered in snow all year round. This isn't true by any means! We are also known as "The Land of the Midnight Sun". June 21st is the Summer Solstice, which is our longest day of the year. In Barrow, Alaska (the most Northern town in Alaska) the sun is in the sky for nearly 60 days! For those of us who are located South of Barrow, Fairbanks will see the sun on June 21st for nearly 22 hours.

Because of this we see that this is reason to celebrate! During the week of June 21st every year we have the Midnight Sun Festival. With the peak of the festival on the Summer Solstice. Across the state and throughout Fairbanks you will find activates centered around the Midnight Sun Festival. These activities include: a 5k run through town, a midnight baseball game with our AAA team the "Gold Panners" and the all out 12-hour street fair! This family-friendly street fair is packed with live music, performances and hundreds of booths selling food, crafts, official festival t-shirts, and handmade souvenirs. Activities include face painting, gold panning, an annual BBQ cook-off, sled dog puppies, and a skate park. This popular block party reflects the importance of summer solstice to Interior Alaskans. With attendance of 30,000+, the Midnight Sun Festival is Alaska's largest single-day event. It's a "don't miss" summer celebration for Fairbanksans and visitors.

24. GOLDEN DAYS FESTIVAL

Head to Fairbanks in the third week of July. That's when residents cut loose in honor of their Gold Rush history, during a five-day festival they call Golden Days! Bank managers dress up as sourdough miners, waitress don "fluzie" outfits, and most of the city turns out for races, parades, and great food. It's a great time to meet locals—who are in a festive, social mood—and to be swept up in a big Alaskan event.

This five-day festival began in 1952, when the Chamber of Commerce decided to honor Fairbanks' Gold Rush and its proud mining tradition. Felix Pedro, a young Italian immigrant, started the rush in 1902 with a gold strike in the foothills outside town.

He's the man who famously proclaimed, "There's gold in them there hills." His cry was heard far and wide: Fairbanks grew from a sleepy river town to a bustling city almost overnight.

The festival includes costume contests, Alaska's largest parade, foot races, a BBQ cook-off, and a rededication of the Felix Pedro monument, which was a gift to Fairbanks from the Italian government.

Most of the events are downtown, just along the Chena River. For the week of the festival, events run pretty much non-stop throughout downtown, at the park, and in other spots. Keep your eyes open for parties; many organizations host events in conjunction with Golden Days.

Festival highlights include:

Grande Parade - Kicking off Saturday morning, the biggest day of the festival, is Alaska's largest parade, complete with some 100 floats, marching bands from across the state, and residents dressed in Gold Rush costumes. The floats have been as intricate as miners panning for gold alongside a running stream. This is a DO NOT MISS event!

Rubber Duckie Race - Held on Saturday, this is one of the biggest events in Fairbanks—not just for Golden Days, but all year! 8,000 rubber ducks are dropped in the Chena River, where they "race" ¼-

mile downstream to the Cushman Bridge. There's $15,000 on the line, plus 80 local prizes, like gift certificates and donated items. Buy a duck for $5, and you could win $5,000. Or buy a duck for $10 and you could win $10,000…but only if your duck is first across the finish line.

Street Fair - On Saturday there is a street fair located on First Avenue and the Golden Heart Plaza. A variety of vendors sell crafts, art, and delicious food to the fair-goers. There is the Kids Korner which hosts free activities for kids such as face painting and pony rides, and there will be entertainment going on throughout the day on the main stage.

River Regatta - The River Regatta is a floatilla of fun! Contestants participate by building crazy and ridiculous rafts and then they attempt to float them down the Chena River. This is always a very entertaining event to witness, and viewers are encouraged to bring water guns to shoot at the participants from the bridge.

Old Tyme Games - This event hosted at Pioneer Park hosts a slew of family friendly activities. From watermelon eating contests, to log splitting, there is a competition for everyone. Felix Pedro makes a special appearance and a local bank weighs his gold nugget for everyone to see.

25. FAIRBANKS SUMMER ARTS FESTIVAL

There are very few art festivals in the country that are as boldly multi-disciplinary as the Fairbanks Summer Arts Festival with classes in music, dance, theatre, visual arts, literary arts, culinary arts, and healing arts.

Fairbanks Summer Arts Festival (FSAF) runs around July 13th-27th. A thousand people, from beginners to advanced practitioners, register each year to explore their inner artist. FSAF brings in 120+ guest artists from around the globe to afford Alaskans the opportunity to learn new artistic techniques and spread their knowledge through instructors.

Whether you want to be part of a drum circle, learn to play the spoons, overcome stage fright, or take your singing to the next level—there's a class for you. One of the most popular classes is one where you will be immersed with professional composers for eight days in the Denali wilderness to focus on sounds in nature.

Fairbanks Summer Arts Festival also offers a multi-day immersive in the visual arts at Chena Hot

Springs. Courses in graphic design, break dancing, and salsa/swing.

Whatever your preference, there is an option to fit nearly every schedule, recently FSAF introduced mini-workshops (sushi, pilates, or glass fusion, anyone?) that only last a few hours on a single afternoon for those constrained by work or travel. This is perfect if you can't stay and enjoy the whole festival but would still like to partake in the festivities!

FSAF also hosts dozens of concerts and performances throughout the two-week festival, including World Music & Dance, Beatles Revue, and American Roots. Perhaps one of the easiest ways to drop in on the festival is via Lunch Bites, a series of free concerts during the lunch hour in places like the Co-Op Plaza, Morris Thompson Cultural and Visitors Center, and Golden Heart Plaza in downtown Fairbanks.

26. WEIO! (WORLD ESKIMO-INDIAN OLYMPICS)

The World Eskimo-Indian Olympics (WEIO) was formed over fifty years ago to spread knowledge and awareness of traditional skills and games to visitors and residents of Alaska. Every summer, top athletes from the circumpolar north (including teams from Greenland and Russia) gather in Fairbanks to compete in tests of strength, endurance, balance, and tolerance for pain. World Eskimo-Indian Olympics usually runs around July 16th-19th at the Carlson Center – located along the Chena River close to downtown.

The games are based on skills prized by Native cultures for thousands of years. The Four Man Carry challenges a single man to carry four people at once for as long as possible, which simulates the heavy packs required to haul meat back to camp after a successful game hunt. The Eskimo Stick Pull replicates the difficulty of pulling a seal out of water by requiring athletes to pull a stick away from their competitor.

The Opening Ceremonies kick off the competitions and welcome all athletes, families, and visitors. The accessibility of WEIO athletes is part of what makes the games such a great experience for spectators. There is no age limit to compete at WEIO, though most athletes are in their late teens or early twenties. Feel free to approach them with questions or congratulations as they walk off the floor, or if you see them hanging around the arena at any point.

WEIO doubles as a cultural celebration with traditional dances and long-standing rituals like the blanket toss (using a blanket made from the hides of 3-4 walrus). The annual Miss WEIO pageant brings young women from across the state to compete in cultural skills and communication.

Eighty vendors exhibit at an annual craft bazaar, which is a great place to hunt for souvenirs. You'll find beaded moccasins, screen-printed sweatshirts, fur hats, and materials like ivory and sealskin that can only legally be used by Native artists.

Elders are granted the highest respect in Native culture and have front row seats at all events. Don't block their view of the arena, if you can help it. Also, it's best to politely request permission if you'd like to take a photo of an individual in the crowd. Group photos or shots of a staged event are fine.

Lastly, don't forget to sample the frybread.

WEIO started as a component of Golden Days, a city-wide celebration of Fairbanks' history, and has since spun off to be it's own nonprofit. It does, however, still coincide with Golden Days, making it easy for visitors to attend both while in town.

27. TAKE A FLIGHT TO OUR CAPITAL!

Alaska is one of the only places I know of where you are unable to access the capital of the state by road. Our capital, Juneau, is one of the islands in the Southeast Panhandle. It is almost closer to Seattle than it is to Fairbanks…not close but you get the picture. If you'd like to visit our great state's capital, you will need to either board a plan or a boat to reach it.

There are not a great number of things to do in small Juneau. However, Mother Nature puts on quite a display for those adventurous enough to go looking in the Last Frontier. While Mendenhall Glacier steals most of the attention and tourist traffic, those who visit Tracy Arm Fjord find the scenery and wildlife unforgettable. For some more accessible natural beauty, head to the Glacier Gardens Rainforest Adventure and breathe in the flower-scented air. One tourist attraction that we are particularly proud of, which is also located indoors, Alaska Brewing Company. Here you can taste a flight of our delicious suds that are all brewed on premise and are distributed across the United States!

28. EXIT GLACIER HIKE

There are few glaciers in Alaska that you can walk right up to, but with Exit Glacier, you can do just that. The walk to the glacier is fairly flat, taking you through a slightly forested area before you end up directly next to the glacier. If you're a moderate hiker, you can take the Upper Trail to the Harding Icefield for a better view of Exit Glacier and the surrounding mountains. Bear in mind that this hike is for those who are very fit and capable, as the climb is both longer and steeper than the easy walk on the lower trail. Also, it is good to remember to make noise while out hiking in Alaska. With our abundance of wildlife, the best way to ward off "natural attention" is to be loud. Growing up in the wilderness, I was always taught to sing, you don't have to be a good singer, but it keeps you loud and makes the hike more enjoyable too!

Distance: 1.8 miles (out and back) – Exit Glacier; 9 miles (out and back) – Harding Icefield Trail

29. WINNER CREEK HIKE

Similar to Exit Glacier, Winner Creek Trail offers an upper and a lower trail with different levels of difficulty. Only 45 minutes outside of Anchorage, this is a nice hike within short travelling distance of the city. The lower trail is 8 miles out and back, with a bridge that crosses the Winner Creek Gorge, and a hand tram that you take across Winner Creek.

This trail is also great for biking, as you can simply load your bike on the tram and take it across the creek. The upper trail turns right at the Gorge and begins its climb there. The trail is roughly 18 miles out and back, so this is a much longer full day hike with more difficult terrain, and the occasional water crossing – dress accordingly.

Distance: 8 miles (out and back) – Lower Trail; 18 miles (out and back) – Upper Trail

30. INSIDE PASSAGE

Shaped by the astounding force of massive glaciers millions of years ago, Alaska's Inside Passage boasts to be one of the best wildlife-filled fjords and lush island sceneries — habitat for bald eagles, sea lions, porpoises and whales. Its mountains are carpeted with majestic forests.

The Inside Passage Alaska is rich with native culture and is home to Tlingit, Haida and Tsimshian Indians whose history is reflected in towering totem poles. As you fly or float through the Passage you will see where Russian settlers left a legacy of onion-domed churches gleaming with icons of the Russian Orthodox church.

To travel the Inside Passage way there are several options depending on your time and budget for your travels. If you are wanting a more local experience, the best way to travel is on the Alaska Marine Highway. This water route will float you to ports along the Inside Passage and can connect you down into Washington, British Columbia or back into the "heartland" of Alaska.

31. SITKA

Sitka is a rather popular stop with many Alaskan cruises. The city of Sitka has such a rich culture and history which visitors from all over the world will enjoy. You will be able to experience the local native cultures through art, food, and festivals, as well as seeing the remanence of when the Russians were infiltrating Southeast Alaska for trade. Sitka is a location also best suited for those looking for adventurous and outdoorsy experience. You will love hiking the area's trails which are thriving with interesting vegetation and wildlife. If you want to meet the wilder residents of Sitka, head to the Alaska Raptor Center, Fortress of the Bear, or Sitka Sound Science Center to get up close and personal with eagles, bears, and salmon. Don't forget to indulge in their local cuisine, which focuses on fresh seafood often caught just hours before it's served to you – hands down the best crab, halibut and salmon you will ever taste! With museums and national parks to art galleries and craft breweries, the time you spend in Sitka will certainly be a memorable one.

32. KETCHIKAN

Ketchikan got its start in early 1900s as a fishing and logging community. Today the 13,000 year-round residents of the town live along a 10 mile stretch of waterfront narrowly spread along the Tongass Narrows. The city is filled with tourists who have come to Ketchikan to fish, hike, kayak, shop, learn more about the Native American culture (especially totems, which are everywhere), or explore the Tongass National Forest or Misty Fjords National Monument. Heads up, Ketchikan is one of the rainiest towns in the USA...yeah it beats Seattle! The town receives an average of 13 feet (152 inches) of rain each year! Over 200 days each year have measurable rain, so don't forget your rain gear!

Be sure to take as stroll along Creek Street, if you have ever watched the movie "The Proposal" this street looks EXACTLY like where they filmed. Other cool, non-Hollywood things about this walk, all the buildings are the original buildings from 1953. You can also visit the oldest building in town here, Dolly's House Museum. Dolly Arthur was Ketchikan's most famous "madam", and the interior of the house looks much like it did in the 1920's. There are many

Alaskan books you can pick up around the shops to learn more about Mrs. Dolly. This is a great way to spend an afternoon, especially if it is raining – which is likely.

Take some time to learn about Totems and the Tlingit culture. Ketchikan is famous for its many totems, and visitors to the town have many opportunities to see them either completed or being carved. There are outdoor totems at Whale Park, near the entrance to Creek Street. The Totem Heritage Center is near the City Park and about a mile or so from downtown. It houses a collection of over 30 original, unrestored totems from Tlingit and Haida villages, most from the 19th century. Saxman village is about 2-3 miles south of Ketchikan, and it has an impressive collection of totems and a cedar community house. This is where you can learn about the Tlingit culture through the songs, dances, and stories. Totem carvers are often at work in the village, and native art is for sale in the shops. The Totem Bight State Park about 10 miles north of Ketchikan is in a beautiful setting, the best way to see this is catch a bus or rent a car for the day. It has numerous totems with good interpretive signs, but no carvers onsite.

The U.S. Forest Service's Southeast Alaska Discovery Center is on Mill Street in downtown Ketchikan. It features exhibits and interactive displays about the land, people, and culture of the region.

Ketchikan has two self-guided walking tours. The first is the downtown walking tour, which takes about two hours or more, depending on how many times you stop to shop or take photos. This walking tour covers the parks, museums, churches, and historic downtown areas like Creek Street. It starts at the Visitors Center and ends just on the other side of the tunnel at the Casey Moran Harbor. The second walk starts at the Harbor View Park (near the end of the downtown walk and continues mostly along the waterfront. This tour is longer, and takes at least 2.5 hours, passing by historic homes and businesses.

33. SKAGWAY

Skagway is a great town to visit. But because of its status as a cruise ship destination, many of the activities are centered around excursions. Have no fear! If you're not looking to spend too much money, there's still plenty of things to do in this Gold Rush town. Like you can take a taste of Skagway's Brewing Company. The popularity of the spruce tip ale means that the Brew Co. is often tapped out, but if you can get your hands on a pint, you won't be disappointed. They use spruce tips instead of hops in this libation. This beer is unique to southeast Alaska, but each of the local breweries puts its own spin on the recipe. The food is also very tasty, and their selection of burgers is awesome. I'm a fan of the Big Kahuna, with pineapple, ham and BBQ sauce.

If you are needing to walk off the food and the brews you should visit the Gold Rush Cemetery. The Gold Rush of 1898 is what put Skagway on the map, and some of the event's less fortunate participants can be found at the north end of town across the White Pass and Yukon Route Railroad tracks. The cemetery is down a short path off the parking lot, and a short walk further brings you to the base of Reid Falls. If you get there at the right time, you can spend a couple minutes waving to the passengers on the WP&YR trains headed up the pass.

One of the must see locations of Skagway is the Red Onion Brothel. There are tours everyday and is

45

an iconic stop since it is the last remining brothel in Skagway from the Gold Rush Days (cause you know there were a heck of a lot more than this one). The tour takes you through the house of ill-repute, as one of its madams leads the way, entertaining you with stories of days gone by. The Red Onion has transformed itself from dance hall bordello to a historic bar & grill, with some of the best food in town if you're so inclined.

34. WATCH THE SALMON RUN AT PULLEN CREEK

The size of the salmon run in Skagway varies yearly. The vast majority of the run is made up of pink salmon, which run every other year. The last big run was 2015, so 2016 might be a small one, but still worth checking out if you are visiting during Salmon Season. For you fishers out there, these are not the salmon you want to catch to eat. As soon as salmon leave the saltwater of the ocean for the freshwater of the streams, they stop eating and their skin begins to decay. Couple that with the fact that pink salmon is usually very oily and not the best to eat anyways, and it's just a waste of time to try and catch them. Still even though you can't fish for them it is still amazing to watch thousands of salmon fight against the current of Pullen Creek as they make their annual migration.

35. HIKE TO YAKUTANIA POINT AND SMUGGLER'S COVE

Skagway has numerous easy day hikes, but they also comprise some of the best things to do in Skagway without spending any money. Yakutania Point and Smuggler's Cove are both short, easy hikes that end at a picturesque point perfect for a picnic lunch or some "scenic drinking."

36. WHITE PASS & YUKON ROUTE RAILWAY

The White Pass and Yukon Route is a Canadian and American narrow-gauge railroad that links Skagway in Alaska and Whitehorse in Yukon. It was built in 1900 during the Klondike Gold Rush – as the fastest way miners could reach the goldfields. It operated until 1982 and was resurrected in 1988 as a heritage railway. It allows passengers to travel back to the past, riding the rails on a real gold rush train,

47

past waterfalls, glacial rivers, steep gorges, and dense forests that have hardly changed since the time of the gold miners.

The train climbs up 3000 feet with passengers aboard parlor cars, both vintage and replicas and with huge windows and observation decks, along the 10-foot-wide train track carved into the mountain. The scenery is breathtaking, and the places the train passes by, such as Dead Horse Gulch or Inspiration Point, fire the imagination and take you all the way up to the headwaters of the legendary Yukon River.

37. KROSCHEL FILMS WILDLIFE CENTER

Located about 28 miles from Haines, Alaska, the Kroschel Films Wildlife Center is an amazing place where filmmaker and naturalist Steve Kroschel takes care of abandoned or orphaned wild animals from Alaska or Canada. It is not a zoo, though, and the animals live free and unmolested in their natural environment, providing you with some perfect photo opportunities as you walk along a well-groomed trail for about 600 yards through the magnificent Alaskan wilderness. Some of the best wildlife photos I've ever taken have been here.

You will encounter 15 species of animals, including grizzly bears, foxes, wolves, lynx, moose, reindeer, owls and others. Steve combines his filmmaking and animal care with a message about the interconnectedness of all life on Earth and natural healing.

38. KODIAK ISLAND, KODIAK

Found on the southern coast off of Alaska, Kodiak Island is the largest amongst the archipelago. The main city, Kodiak, is the hub from which all connections with the rest of the world go through and will be your starting point when exploring this wondrous location. Having originally been inhabited by Alutiiq natives for over 7,000 years, and then the short-lived home of the Russian Crown, there is so much history and culture here. Spend your time exploring the outdoors at one of their many state parks, where you'll surely come across wildlife such as their bear population, deer, elk, seals, whales, eagles, and more.

39. ALUTIIQ MUSEUM – KODIAK

To preserve, explore, and celebrate the culture of Native Alutiiq communities, the Kodiak Area Native Association's Culture and Heritage Division established several island-wide programs dedicated to sharing the Alutiiq language, art, and history. Through their many displays, you'll be able to learn about the Alutiiq/ Sugpiaq people, indigenous plants, and about their native language. There is always something new to see with several temporary exhibits and workshops that come through the museum, including a hands-on exploration of Alutiiq arts which may be displayed in their growing gallery.

40. KODIAK MILITARY HISTORY MUSEUM

Attracting veterans and visitors from all over, the Kodiak Military History Museum has several displays and exhibits dedicated to the land's military heroes and history. The museum itself is housed in Fort Abercrombie's Ready Ammunition Bunker. The bunker, located at Miller Point, was built by Navy SeaBees of CB-43 in 1943. Within and surrounding the building, visitors will be able to see the remains of two eight-inch gun mounts, several gun barrels, and many other aspects. Several of the artifacts on display there include model telephones, typewriters, newspapers, artillery shells, vehicles, uniforms, and more.

41. KODIAK WILDLIFE TOURS

Kodiak Wildlife Tours offers a range of day tours for visitors who want to explore the stunning sights and wildlife of the area but don't know where to start. The experienced professionals only conduct one tour a day, each lasting from four to five hours, and only accommodate small groups of four to five people so that everyone has an enjoyable experience that is personalized and dedicated to them. You may be able to see bald eagles, pacific salmon, sea otters, and Kodiak brown bears. All of their tours, whether it be a nature walk, for wildlife viewing, or photography-focused, comes with a gourmet lunch filled with local flavors and treats.

42. BIGGEST FOR LAST – ANCHORAGE!

As with all of Alaska, proximity to the great outdoors is the most obvious reason to visit Anchorage. The city is just a short drive from major hiking spots, ski areas and national parks, so stretch your legs along the popular Tony Knowles Coastal Trail or cast your line for dinner at salmon-swamped Ship Creek. But don't be too quick to head out of town, though; Anchorage hosts numerous fascinating and family-friendly attractions. If you're an avid museum-goer, make some time for the Alaska Aviation Museum or, if you've got little ones in tow, the Alaska Native Heritage Center is home to interactive exhibits that spotlight Alaska's history and culture.

43. ANCHORAGE MARKET & FESTIVAL

This market is a local favorite since it first opened in 1992, the Anchorage Market and Festival started out as a Saturday-only market with just two dozen vendors, but it quickly grew to host more than 300 vendors and now also operates on Sundays. Located on 7 acres in downtown Anchorage, this is the place to shop for clothes, food, crafts and more while enjoying live entertainment and snacking on locally grown eats. There's also a kid's market suitable for ages 8 to 16 that sells goods crafted by other youngsters.

Recent visitors spoke highly of the quality and quantity of unique wares, gifts and local food available at the market, while others warned that finding parking can be a challenge. Plan ahead and take public transportation: People Mover route Nos. 13 and 15 drop passengers off a couple blocks from the market, which is located at the intersection of 3rd and E Street. The market is open from mid-May to September on Saturdays from 10 a.m. to 6 p.m. and on Sundays from 10 a.m. to 5 p.m.

44. ALASKA ZOO

If during your trip you missed out on seeing some of our natural wildlife, visit them (safely) at the Alaska Zoo. This zoo rescues numerous critters – including moose, caribou, polar bears, seals and wolves, among others – that can no longer survive in the wild. Anchorage's residents hold this quaint zoo close to their hearts – they have even named all the animals housed there. I grew up going to the Alaska Zoo at least once a year to visit the Polar Bears

You'll find the Alaska Zoo sitting southeast of downtown along O'Malley Road. The animals welcome visitors every day, although hours vary depending on the season. Admission is $15 for adults and $7 for children.

45. ALASKA TROOPER MUSEUM

Have you ever watched the "Alaska State Trooper" show? Well here is a condensed history of the show…in real life. How would you police a wild frontier? Alaska has a long and interesting history with law enforcement, including a cooperative agreement with the Canadian Mounties, and the Alaska Trooper Museum tells all the tales. Plus, there's a forensic science camp and a Hudson Hornet.

46. GEOCACHING

Treasure hunting is alive and well with geocaching. Anchorage is covered with little hidden treasures. Use your GPS or smart phone to find fun clues left by visitors and locals before you, then add your own clues to the adventure. The Anchorage Log Cabin Information Center offers a geocaching guide. It is like a Pokémon game in real life.

47. KINCAID GRILL AND WINE BAR

This is where you will find the finest in food preparation and uncompromising service. Kincaid Grill is located in a quiet West Anchorage neighborhood which lends itself to its unique sense of personal touches. Kincaid Grill is well known for being one of the finest restaurants in the Anchorage area for its quality preparation of what we call Alaskan Regional cuisine. This is fairly expensive place to eat but if you wanted to plan a nice date night or evening while in Anchorage.

48. ULU FACTORY

If you visit Anchorage as part of a tour group, they will almost certainly get you to see the Ulu factory. If you aren't on a tour, you should venture here anyways. Here you will get to see how the traditional ulu knife is made and encouraged to buy it as a gift to your friends and family. The "factory" tour also includes an instructional talk about caring for ulu knives, how to sharpen it, how to use it etc.

During the months of July and August, the Ulu Factory offers visitors free rides in their vintage trolley from downtown Anchorage to the factory. Expect the place to be busy, especially if there's a large group coming in from one of the cruise ships. Opening Hours: Sundays through Saturdays from 10:00 A.M. to 7:00 P.M.

49. 49TH STATE BREWING COMPANY

At the 49th State-Anchorage, the cultural layers of Alaska unfold around you, both in the atmosphere and the food. Here, you can delve into the long tradition of brewing with our award-winning beer, explore a menu filled with freshly sourced Alaskan products, or relax on the rooftop patio overlooking the Cook Inlet and Alaska Range. With an environment welcoming to locals and tourists alike, there's something for everyone.

50. EKLUTNA VILLAGE HISTORICAL PARK

Getting there takes a 30-minute drive but it is well worth the trip and if you have a car, add it to your own list of things to do in Anchorage. Visiting the park, you will get to see and learn about the history, culture, and customs of the Dena'ina Athabascans and how Russian Orthodox traditions influenced them.

One of the interesting things to see at the Eklutna Village Historic Park is the Spirit Houses, which are unique to Athabaskan tradition. Per the cultural beliefs, these houses were built by families of persons who already died, and this serves as marking of the deceased person's grave.

Free parking is provided so the only thing to worry about is the admission fee. There's some walking to do around the place, so wear comfortable shoes, bring rain gear (just in case) and don't forget bug spray. It is only open to the public from May 15 through September 15; The guided tours are from Monday through Fridays from 10:00 A.M. to 5:00 P.M.

TOP REASONS TO BOOK THIS TRIP

Native Culture: There are 229 federally recognized Alaska Native villages. You will be hard pressed to not find some culture during your visit. It is all around you! In our buildings, our food, names and art work – it is all around you.

Breathe Taking Landscapes: As a photographer growing up in Alaska, I always used to joke by saying "I was privy to some of the best landscapes in the world to learn how to be a photographer. And if I couldn't learn there – there was no learning for me." It doesn't matter what time year you come to visit, summer and endless daylight or in the winter when everything is a winter wonderland.

Wildlife/Outdoors Activities: Most of Alaska is still wild, there are many villages that you can't access unless you are flying a Bush plane out to them. This means that everything around you is wild – so if you crave a walk on the wild side or wanting to take a break away from the busy life of the "big city" -

Visiting Alaska is just the place for you to get in touch with your inner explorer!

OTHER RESOURCES:

www.alaskatrain.com

https://www.nps.gov/dena/index.htm

BONUS BOOK

50 THINGS TO KNOW ABOUT PACKING LIGHT FOR TRAVEL

PACK THE RIGHT WAY EVERY TIME

AUTHOR: MANIDIPA BHATTACHARYYA

Edited by Melanie Howthorne

ABOUT THE AUTHOR

Manidipa Bhattacharyya is a creative writer and editor, with an education in English literature and Linguistics. After working in the IT industry for seven long years she decided to call it quits and follow her heart instead. Manidipa has been ghost writing, editing, proof reading and doing secondary research services for many story tellers and article writers for about three years. She stays in Kolkata, India with her husband and a busy two year old. In her own time Manidipa enjoys travelling, photography and writing flash fiction.

Manidipa believes in travelling light and never carries anything that she couldn't haul herself on a trip. However, travelling with her child changed the scenario. She seemed to carry the entire world with her for the baby on the first two trips. But good sense prevailed and she is again working her way to becoming a light traveler, this time with a kid.

INTRODUCTION

He who would travel happily
must travel light.

-Antoine de Saint-Exupéry

Travel takes you to different places from seas and mountains to deserts and much more. In your travels you get to interact with different people and their cultures. You will, however, enjoy the sights and interact positively with these new people even more, if you are travelling light.

When you travel light your mind can be free from worry about your belongings. You do not have to spend precious vacation time waiting for your luggage to arrive after a long flight. There is be no chance of your bags going missing and the best part is that you need not pay a fee for checked baggage.

People who have mastered this art of packing light will root for you to take only one carry-on, wherever you go. However, many people can find it really hard to pack light. More so if you are travelling with children. Differentiating between "must have" and "just in case" items is the starting point. There will be ample shopping avenues at your destination which are just waiting to be explored.

63

This book will show you 'packing' in a new 'light' –
pun intended – and help you to embrace light
packing practices for all of your future travels.

Off to packing!

DEDICATION

I dedicate this book to all the travel buffs that I know,
who have given me great insights into the contents of
their backpacks.

THE RIGHT TRAVEL GEAR

1. CHOOSE YOUR TRAVEL GEAR CAREFULLY

While selecting your travel gear, pick items that are
light weight, durable and most importantly, easy to
carry. There are cases with wheels so you can drag
them along – these are usually on the heavy side
because of the trolley. Alternatively a backpack that
you can carry comfortably on your back, or even a
duffel bag that you can carry easily by hand or sling
across your body are also great options. Whatever
you choose, one thing to keep in mind is that the
luggage itself should not weigh a ton, this will give
you the flexibility to bring along one extra pair of
shoes if you so desire.

2. CARRY THE MINIMUM NUMBER OF BAGS

Selecting light weight luggage is not everything. You need to restrict the number of bags you carry as well. One carry-on size bag is ideal for light travel. Most carriers allow one cabin baggage plus one purse, handbag or camera bag as long as it slides under the seat in front. So technically, you can carry two items of luggage without checking them in.

3. PACK ONE EXTRA BAG

Always pack one extra empty bag along with your essential items. This could be a very light weight duffel bag or even a sturdy tote bag which takes up minimal space. In the event that you end up buying a lot of souvenirs, you already have a handy bag to stuff all that into and do not have to spend time hunting for an appropriate bag.

I'm very strict with my packing and have everything in its right place. I never change a rule. I hardly use anything in the hotel room. I wheel my own wardrobe in and that's it.

Charlie Watts

CLOTHES & ACCESSORIES

4. PLAN AHEAD

Figure out in advance what you plan to do on your trip. That will help you to pick that one dress you need for the occasion. If you are going to attend a wedding then you have to carry formal wear. If not, you can ditch the gown for something lighter that will be comfortable during long walks or on the beach.

5. WEAR THAT JACKET

Remember that wearing items will not add extra luggage for your air travel. So wear that bulky jacket that you plan to carry for your trip. This saves space and can also help keep you warm during the chilly flight.

6. MIX AND MATCH

Carry clothes that can be interchangeably used to reinvent your look. Find one top that goes well with a couple of pairs of pants or skirts. Use tops, shirts and jackets wisely along with other accessories like a scarf or a stole to create a new look.

7. CHOOSE YOUR FABRIC WISELY

Stuffing clothes in cramped bags definitely takes its toll which results in wrinkles. It is best to carry wrinkle free, synthetic clothes or merino tops. This will eliminate the need for that small iron you usually bring along.

8. DITCH CLOTHES PACK UNDERWEAR

Pack more underwear and socks. These are the things that will give you a fresh feel even if you do not get a chance to wear fresh clothes. Moreover these are easy to wash and can be dried inside the hotel room itself.

9. CHOOSE DARK OVER LIGHT

While picking your clothes choose dark coloured ones. They are easy to colour coordinate and can last longer before needing a wash. Accidental food spills and dirt from the road are less visible on darker clothes.

10. WEAR YOUR JEANS

Take only one pair of Jeans with you, which you should wear on the flight. Remember to pick a pair that can be worn for sightseeing trips and is equally eloquent for dinner. You can add variety by adding light weight cargoes and chinos.

11. CARRY SMART ACCESSORIES

The right accessory can give you a fresh look even with the same old dress. An intelligent neck-piece, a couple of bright scarves, stoles or a sarong can be used in a number of ways to add variety to your clothing. These light weight beauties can double up as a nursing cover, a light blanket, beach wear, a modesty cover for visiting places of worship, and also makes for an enthralling game of peek-a-boo.

12. LEARN TO FOLD YOUR GARMENTS

Seasoned travellers all swear by rolling their clothes for compact and wrinkle free packing. Bundle packing, where you roll the clothes around a central object as if tying it up, is also a popular method of compact and wrinkle free packing. Stacking folded clothes one on top of another is a big no-no as it makes creases extreme and they are difficult to get rid of without ironing.

13. WASH YOUR DIRTY LAUNDRY

One of the ways to avoid carrying loads of clothes is to wash the clothes you carry. At some places you might get to use the laundry services or a Laundromat but if you are in a pinch, best solution is to wash them yourself. If that is the plan then carrying quick drying clothes is highly recommended, which most often also happen to be the wrinkle free variety.

14. LEAVE THOSE TOWELS BEHIND

Regular towels take up a lot of space, are heavy and take ages to dry out. If you are staying at hotels they will provide you with towels anyway. If you are travelling to a remote place, where the availability of towels look doubtful, carry a light weight travel towel of viscose material to do the job.

15. USE A COMPRESSION BAG

Compression bags are getting lots of recommendation now days from regular travellers. These are useful for saving space in your luggage when you have to pack bulky dresses. While packing for the return trip, get help from the hotel staff to arrange a vacuum cleaner.

FOOTWEAR

16. PUT ON YOUR HIKING BOOTS

If you have plans to go hiking or trekking during your trip, you will need those bulky hiking boots. The best way to carry them is to wear them on flight to save space and luggage weight. You can remove the boots once inside and be comfortable in your socks.

17. PICKING THE RIGHT SHOES

Shoes are often the bulkiest items, along with being the dainty if you are a female. They need care and take up a lot of space in your luggage. It is advisable therefore to pick shoes very carefully. If you plan to do a lot of walking and site seeing, then wearing a pair of comfortable walking shoes are a must. For more formal occasions you can carry durable, light weight flats which will not take up much space.

18. STUFF SHOES

If you happen to pack a pair of shoes, ensure you utilize their hollow insides. Tuck small items like rolled up socks or belts to save space. They will also be easy to find.

TOILETRIES

19. STASHING TOILETRIES

Carry only absolute necessities. Airline rules dictate
that for one carry-on bag, liquids and gels must be in
3.4 ounce (100ml) bottles or less, and must be packed
in a one quart zip-lock bag. If you are planning to stay
in a hotel, the basic things will be provided for you.
It's best is to buy the rest from the local market at
your destination.

20. TAKE ALONG TAMPONS

Tampons are a hard to find item in a lot of countries.
Figure out how many you need and pack accordingly.
For longer stays you can buy them online and have
them delivered to where you are staying.

21. GET PAMPERED BEFORE YOU TRAVEL

Some avid travellers suggest getting a pedicure and
manicure just the day before travelling. This not only
gives you a well kept look, you also save the trouble
of packing nail polish. Remember, every little bit of
weight reduced adds up.

ELECTRONICS

22. LUGGING ALONG ELECTRONICS

Electronics have a large role to play in our lives today. Most of us cannot imagine our lives away from our phones, laptops or tablets. However while travelling, one must consider the amount of weight these electronics add to our luggage. Thankfully smart phones come along with all the essentials tools like a camera, email access, picture editing tools and more. They are smart to the point of eliminating the need to carry multiple gadgets. Choose a smart phone that suits all your requirements and travel with the world in your palms or pocket.

23. REDUCE THE NUMBER OF CHARGERS

If you do travel with multiple electronic devices, you will have to bear the additional burden of carrying all their chargers too. Check if a single charger can be used for multiple devices. You might also consider investing in a pocket charger. These small devices support multiple devices while keeping you charged on the go.

24. TRAVEL FRIENDLY APPS

Along with smart phones come numerous apps, which are immensely helpful in our travels. You name it and you have an app for it at hand – take pictures, sharing with friends and family, torch to light dark roads, maps, checking flight/train times, find hotels and many other things. Use these smart alternatives to traditional items like books to eliminate weight and save space.

I get ideas about what's essential when packing my suitcase.

-Diane von Furstenberg

TRAVELLING WITH KIDS

25. BRING ALONG THE STROLLER

Kids might enjoy walking for a while but they soon tire out and a stroller is the just the right thing for them to rest in while you continue your tour. Strollers also double duty as a luggage carrier and shopping bag holder. Remember to pick a light weight, easy to handle brand of stroller. Better yet, find out in advance if you can rent a stroller at your destination.

26. BRING ONLY ENOUGH DIAPERS FOR YOUR TRIP

Diapers take up a lot of space and add to the weight of your luggage. Therefore it is advisable to carry just enough diapers to last through the trip and a few for afterwards, till you buy fresh stock at your destination. Unless of course you are travelling to a really remote area, in which case you have no choice but to carry the load. Otherwise diapers are something you will find pretty easily.

27. TAKE ONLY A COUPLE OF TOYS

Children are easily attracted by new things in their environment. While travelling they will find numerous 'new' objects to scrutinize and play with. Packing just one favorite toy is enough, or if there is no favorite toy leave out all of them in favor of stories or imaginary games.

28. CARRY KID FRIENDLY SNACKS

Create a small snack counter in your bag to store away quick bites for those sudden hunger pangs. Depending on the child's age this could include chocolates, raisins, dry fruits, granola bars or biscuits. Also keep a bottle of water handy for your little one.

These things do not add much weight and can be adjusted in a handbag or knapsack.

29. GAMES TO CARRY

Create some travel specific, imaginary games if you have slightly grown up children, like spot the attractions. Keep a coloring book and colors handy for in-flight or hotel time. Apps on your smart phone can keep the children engaged with cartoons and story books. Older children are often entertained by games available on phones or tablets. This cuts the weight of luggage down while keeping the kids entertained.

30. LET THE KIDS CARRY THEIR LOAD

A good thing is to start early sharing of responsibilities. Let your child pick a bag of his or her choice and pack it themselves. Keep tabs on what they are stuffing in their bags by asking if they will be using that item on the trip. It could start out being just an entertainment bag initially but with growing years they will learn to sort the useful from the superfluous. Children as little as four can maneuver a small trolley suitcase like a pro- their experience in pull along toys credit. If you are worried that you may be pulling it for them, you may want to start with a backpack.

31. DECIDE ON LOCATION FOR CHILDREN TO SLEEP

While on a trip you might not always get a crib at your destination, and carrying one will make life all the more difficult. Instead call ahead to see if there are any cribs or roll out beds for children. You may even put blankets on the floor. Weave them a story about camping and they will gladly sleep without any trouble.

32. GET BABY PRODUCTS DELIVERED AT YOUR DESTINATION

If you are absolutely paranoid about not getting your favourite variety of diaper or brand of baby food, check out online stores like amazon.com for services in your destination city. You can buy things online ahead of your travel and get them delivered to your hotel upon arrival.

33. FEEDING NEEDS OF YOUR INFANTS

If you are travelling with a breastfed infant, you save the trouble of carrying bottles and bottle sanitization kits. For special food, or medications, you may need to call ahead to make sure you have a refrigerator where you are staying.

34. FEEDING NEEDS OF YOUR TODDLER

With the progression from infancy to toddler, their dietary requirements too evolve. You will have to pack some snacks for travelling time. Fresh fruits and vegetables can be purchased at your destination. Most of the cities you travel to in whichever part of the world, will have baby food products and formulas, available at the local drug-store or the supermarket.

35. PICKING CLOTHES FOR YOUR BABY

Contrary to popular belief, babies can do without many changes of clothes. At the most pack 2 outfits per day. Pack mix and match type clothes for your little one as well. Pick things which are comfortable to wear and quick to dry.

36. SELECTING SHOES FOR YOUR BABY

Like outfits, kids can make do with two pairs of comfortable shoes. If you can get some water resistant shoes it will be best. To expedite drying wet shoes, you can stuff newspaper in them then wrap them with newspaper and leave them to dry overnight.

37. KEEP ONE CHANGE OF CLOTHES HANDY

Travelling with kids can be tricky. Keep a change of clothes for the kids and mum handy in your purse or tote bag. This takes a bit of space in your hand luggage but comes extremely handy in case there are any accidents or spills.

38. LEAVE BEHIND BABY ACCESSORIES

Baby accessories like their bed, bath tub, car seat, crib etc. should be left at home. Many hotels provide a crib on request, while car seats can be borrowed from friends or rented. Babies can be given a bath in the hotel sink or even in the adult bath tub with a little bit of water. If you bring a few bath toys, they can be used in the bath, pool, and out of water. They can also be sanitized easily in the sink.

39. CARRY A SMALL LOAD OF PLASTIC BAGS

With children around there are chances of a number of soiled clothes and diapers. These plastic bags help to sort the dirt from the clean inside your big bag.

These are very light weight and come in handy to other carry stuff as well at times.

PACK WITH A PURPOSE

40. PACKING FOR BUSINESS TRIPS

One neutral-colored suit should suffice. It can be paired with different shirts, ties and accessories for different occasions. One pair of black suit pants could be worn with a matching jacket for the office or with a snazzy top for dinner.

41. PACKING FOR A CRUISE

Most cruises have formal dinners, and that formal dress usually takes up a lot of space. However you might find a tuxedo to rent. For women, a short black dress with multiple accessory options will do the trick.

42. PACKING FOR A LONG TRIP OVER DIFFERENT CLIMATES

The secret packing mantra for travel over multiple climates is layering. Layering traps air around your body creating insulation against the cold. The same light t-shirt that is comfortable in a warmer climate can be the innermost layer in a colder climate.

REDUCE SOME MORE WEIGHT

43. LEAVE PRECIOUS THINGS AT HOME

Things that you would hate to lose or get damaged leave them at home. Precious jewelry, expensive gadgets or dresses, could be anything. You will not require these on your trip. Leave them at home and spare the load on your mind.

44. SEND SOUVENIRS BY MAIL

If you have spent all your money on purchasing souvenirs, carrying them back in the same bag that you brought along would be difficult. Either pack everything in another bag and check it in the airport or get everything shipped to your home. Use an international carrier for a secure transit, but this could be more expensive than the checking fees at the airport.

45. AVOID CARRYING BOOKS

Books equal to weight. There are many reading apps which you can download on your smart phone or tab.

Plus there are gadgets like Kindle and Nook that are thinner and lighter alternatives to your regular book.

CHECK, GET, SET, CHECK AGAIN

46. STRATEGIZE BEFORE PACKING

Create a travel list and prepare all that you think you need to carry along. Keep everything on your bed or floor before packing and then think through once again – do I really need that? Any item that meets this question can be avoided. Remove whatever you don't really need and pack the rest.

47. TEST YOUR LUGGAGE

Once you have fully packed for the trip take a test trip with your luggage. Take your bags and go to town for window shopping for an hour. If you enjoy your hour long trip it is good to go, if not, go home and reduce the load some more. Repeat this test till you hit the right weight.

48. ADD A ROLL OF DUCT TAPE

You might wonder why, when this book has been talking about reducing stuff, we're suddenly asking you to pack something totally unusual. This is because when you have limited supplies, duct tape is immensely helpful for small repairs – a broken bag, leaking zip-lock bag, broken sunglasses, you name it and duct tape can fix it, temporarily.

49. LIST OF ESSENTIAL ITEMS

Even though the emphasis is on packing light, there are things which have to be carried for any trip. Here is our list of essentials:

•Passport/Visa or any other ID

•Any other paper work that might be required on a trip like permits, hotel reservation confirmations etc.

•Medicines – all your prescription medicines and emergency kit, especially if you are travelling with children

•Medical or vaccination records

•Money in foreign currency if travelling to a different country

•Tickets- Email or Message them to your phone

50. MAKE THE MOST OF YOUR TRIP

Wherever you are going, whatever you hope to do we encourage you to embrace it whole-heartedly. Take in the scenery, the culture and above all, enjoy your time away from home.

On a long journey even a straw weighs heavy.

-Spanish Proverb

PACKING AND PLANNING TIPS

A Week before Leaving

- Arrange for someone to take care of pets and water plants.

- Stop mail and newspaper.

- Notify Credit Card companies where you are going.

- Change your thermostat settings.

- Car inspected, oil is changed, and tires have the correct pressure.

- Passports and photo identification is up to date.

- Pay bills.

- Copy important items and download travel Apps.

- Start collecting small bills for tips.

Right Before Leaving

- Clean out refrigerator.

- Empty garbage cans.

- Lock windows.

- Make sure you have the proper identification with you.

- Bring cash for tips.

- Remember travel documents.

- Lock door behind you.

- Remember wallet.

- Unplug items in house and pack chargers.

>TOURIST

READ OTHER
GREATER THAN A TOURIST
BOOKS

Greater Than a Tourist San Miguel de Allende Guanajuato Mexico:
50 Travel Tips from a Local by Tom Peterson

Greater Than a Tourist – Lake George Area New York USA:
 50 Travel Tips from a Local by Janine Hirschklau

Greater Than a Tourist – Monterey California United States:
50 Travel Tips from a Local by Katie Begley

 Greater Than a Tourist – Chanai Crete Greece:
50 Travel Tips from a Local by Dimitra Papagrigoraki

Greater Than a Tourist – The Garden Route Western Cape Province
South Africa: 50 Travel Tips from a Local by Li-Anne McGregor van
Aardt

Greater Than a Tourist – Sevilla Andalusia Spain:
50 Travel Tips from a Local by Gabi Gazon

Greater Than a Tourist – Kota Bharu Kelantan Malaysia:
50 Travel Tips from a Local by Aditi Shukla

Children's Book: Charlie the Cavalier Travels the World by Lisa
Rusczyk

>TOURIST

> TOURIST

Visit Greater Than a Tourist for Free Travel Tips
http://GreaterThanATourist.com

Sign up for the Greater Than a Tourist Newsletter for discount days, new books, and travel information:
http://eepurl.com/cxspyf

Follow us on Facebook for tips, images, and ideas:
https://www.facebook.com/GreaterThanATourist

Follow us on Pinterest for travel tips and ideas:
http://pinterest.com/GreaterThanATourist

Follow us on Instagram for beautiful travel images:
http://Instagram.com/GreaterThanATourist

> TOURIST

Please leave your honest review of this book on Amazon and Goodreads. Please send your feedback to GreaterThanaTourist@gmail.com as we continue to improve the series. We appreciate your positive and constructive feedback. Thank you.

METRIC CONVERSIONS

TEMPERATURE

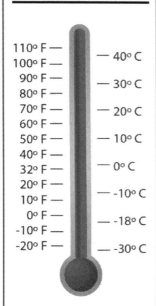

110° F —	— 40° C
100° F —	
90° F —	— 30° C
80° F —	
70° F —	— 20° C
60° F —	
50° F —	— 10° C
40° F —	
32° F —	— 0° C
20° F —	
10° F —	— -10° C
0° F —	
-10° F —	— -18° C
-20° F —	— -30° C

To convert F to C:

Subtract 32, and then multiply
by 5/9 or .5555.

To Convert C to F:

Multiply by 1.8
and then add 32.

32F = 0C

LIQUID VOLUME

To Convert:..................Multiply by
U.S. Gallons to Liters................. 3.8
U.S. Liters to Gallons 26
Imperial Gallons to U.S. Gallons 1.2
Imperial Gallons to Liters....... 4.55
Liters to Imperial Gallons 22
1 Liter = .26 U.S. Gallon
1 U.S. Gallon = 3.8 Liters

DISTANCE

To convert ....Multiply by
Inches to Centimeters 2.54
Centimeters to Inches 39
Feet to Meters...................... .3
Meters to Feet 3.28
Yards to Meters 91
Meters to Yards 1.09
Miles to Kilometers 1.61
Kilometers to Miles............ .62
1 Mile = 1.6 km
1 km = .62 Miles

WEIGHT

1 Ounce = .28 Grams
1 Pound = .4555 Kilograms
1 Gram = .04 Ounce
1 Kilogram = 2.2 Pounds

93

TRAVEL QUESTIONS

- Do you bring presents home to family or friends after a vacation?

- Do you get motion sick?

- Do you have a favorite billboard?

- Do you know what to do if there is a flat tire?

- Do you like a sun roof open?

- Do you like to eat in the car?

- Do you like to wear sun glasses in the car?

- Do you like toppings on your ice cream?

- Do you use public bathrooms?

- Did you bring your cell phone and does it have power?

- Do you have a form of identification with you?

- Have you ever been pulled over by a cop?

- Have you ever given money to a stranger on a road trip?

- Have you ever taken a road trip with animals?

- Have you ever went on a vacation alone?

- Have you ever run out of gas?

- If you could move to any place in the world, where would it be?

- If you could travel anywhere in the world, where would you travel?

- If you could travel in any vehicle, which one would it be?

- If you had three things to wish for from a magic genie, what would they be?

- If you have a driver's license, how many times did it take you to pass the test?

- What are you the most afraid of on vacation?

- What do you want to get away from the most when you are on vacation?

- What foods smells bad to you?

- What item do you bring on ever trip with you away from home?

- What makes you sleepy?

- What song would you love to hear on the radio when you're cruising on the highway?

- What travel job would you want the least?

- What will you miss most while you are away from home?

- What is something you always wanted to try?

- What is the best road side attraction that you ever saw?

- What is the farthest distance you ever biked?

- What is the farthest distance you ever walked?

- What is the weirdest thing you needed to buy while on vacation?

- What is your favorite candy?

- What is your favorite color car?

- What is your favorite family vacation?

- What is your favorite food?

- What is your favorite gas station drink or food?

- What is your favorite license plate design?

- What is your favorite restaurant?

- What is your favorite smell?

- What is your favorite song?

- What is your favorite sound that nature makes?

- What is your favorite thing to bring home from a vacation?

- What is your favorite vacation with friends?

- What is your favorite way to relax?

- Where is the farthest place you ever traveled in a car?

- Where is the farthest place you ever went North, South, East and West?

- Where is your favorite place in the world?

- Who is your favorite singer?

- Who taught you how to drive?

- Who will you miss the most while you are away?

- Who if the first person you will contact when you get to your destination?

- Who brought you on your first vacation?

- Who likes to travel the most in your life?

- Would you rather be hot or cold?

- Would you rather drive above, below, or at the speed limited?

- Would you rather drive on a highway or a back road?

- Would you rather go on a train or a boat?

- Would you rather go to the beach or the woods?

TRAVEL BUCKET LIST

1.

2.

3.

4.

5.

6.

7.

8.

9.

10.

NOTES

Manufactured by Amazon.ca
Bolton, ON